My Little Kitten Care Guide

Author: Sean M
Designe
Cat Breed Phot

tangerine
Press
an imprint of
SCHOLASTIC
www.scholastic.com

Scholastic and Tangerine Press and associated logos are trademarks of Scholastic Inc
Published by Tangerine Press, an imprint of Scholastic Inc; 557 Broadway;
New York, NY 10012
10 9 8 7 6 5 4 3 2 1
ISBN: 0-439-73670-6
Printed and bound in China

Did you just get your first cat? You must be really excited. This book is where you find out how to be the purrrfect cat owner!

Cats are cute and cuddly, but they are not toys. They need love, attention, and someone to feed and take care of them.

This book tells you how to keep your kitty healthy and happy. Find out how cats communicate, how they stay clean, and what they like to eat. And if you don't have a kitty yet, see what kind might be best for you. You'll be amazed by all the different kinds of cats! They come in all different shapes, sizes, fur lengths, patterns, and colors.

Over six thousand years ago many people believed cats were sacred animals. Ancient Egyptians thought the sun's rays were kept inside cat eyes, because they glow in the dark. Killing a cat was punishable by death in Ancient Egypt, and families would shave their eyebrows as a sign of sadness if their cat died.

Along with many true stories about cats, there are hundreds of myths and superstitions. Have you heard that a black cat crossing your path means bad luck? That superstition comes from the Middle Ages. People believed a black cat would bring poverty and misfortune.

Many people felt that a cat's powers were so strong a person who harmed a cat would have horrible bad luck, or worse! Early Christians believed cats were linked with the devil and witches, and tried to avoid them at all costs. Today, cats are mainly considered friendly, sweet, and playful animals that are fun to watch and even more fun to cuddle. There is even scientific research that shows how petting a cat can help you relax.

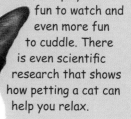

Your kitty's walk, expressions, and ways of playing/hunting are almost exactly like a lion's or a tiger's.

Cat Facts!

- ❧ Cats make over one hundred different voice sounds! Dogs don't make close to that many.
- ❧ Cats see about six times better at night than humans do!
- ❧ Americans spend more money on cat food than on baby food! Amazing!
- ❧ The heaviest pet cat weighed about 47 lbs. (21 kg). Can you believe it?

- ❧ Cats don't have collarbones. That's why, even with 230 bones in its body, a cat can fit through any space that its head fits through. WOW!
- ❧ Cats sleep between 16 and 18 hours a day! Wouldn't it be nice to sleep that long?
- ❧ Cats have five toes on each front paw, but they have four on each back paw!
- ❧ Cats are not colorblind. They can see green, blue, and red!

- ❧ Cat's smell with their nose, but also with the Jacobsen's organ. This is in the top part of a cat's mouth. Cool, huh?
- ❧ Cat urine glows under a black light! Eeewwww! Did you want to know that?

Feeding your cat

A cat can't see directly under its nose, which is why it can't find tiny treats dropped on the floor.

Like lions, cats eat mostly meat, so half of a cat's diet should be meat and the other half should be veggies. Pet cats get a balanced diet from ready-made cat food. Using both wet and dry food is best, but if you use only dry food make sure your cat has plenty of water.

Check the label on cat food. The first ingredient should be fish, lamb, or chicken. The best way to make sure your cat eats right and stays healthy is to feed it only cat food. Some foods can make a cat sick. Even milk can be bad for a cat, if it has too much. If you do want to give your kitty people food, be sure it doesn't have sugar and NEVER give a cat chocolate! Even a little bit could kill your cat!

It's a good idea to use glass, metal, or ceramic food and water bowls, because cats can have allergies to plastic ones.

Cats can be fussy eaters, but they can also eat too much. Check with your vet to see what is a good weight for your kitty. If your cat is a fussy eater, warm up some wet food in a microwaveable dish. Put it in for about ten seconds and test the temperature with your pinky finger.

Hairballs

Your cat may get hairballs. You'll hear it making coughing noises. Don't worry! Cats get hairballs all the time. If your cat gets them, buy some grass at the pet store to help with digestion. You can also give your cat hairball medicine or about 1/8 tsp. of vaseline.

Vet Visits

Cats need to go for a yearly checkup and shots, just like people. The vet will look your cat over from head to tail. The vet will also check for internal parasites and worms.

If your cat stops eating, doesn't move much, or starts act-ing strange or a little. mean, these can be signs that something is wrong with it. Take your kitty to the vet. Your cat relies on you to tell the vet what's been happening.

CHEMICALS CAN BE ABSORBED THROUGH A CAT'S PAWS. FLOOR WAXES AND OTHER PRODUCTS CAN BE DANGEROUS. SO DON'T LET YOUR CAT WALK ON THE FLOOR WHEN YOU'RE CLEANING IT.

Dental Health

Just like you, your cat's teeth need brushing. However, you need to do the brushing for your friend by using a kitty toothbrush and kitty toothpaste. Put a little of the toothpaste on your finger to let your cat taste it. After doing this a few times, softly brush just one or two teeth, making a circle with the brush. Over the next few weeks, you can brush more teeth when your cat feels more comfortable. Remember to brush the back teeth.

Brush your cat's teeth each week. Always be gentle when brushing and stop if your cat begins to fuss. When your cat has had all of its teeth brushed, give it a treat made to prevent tartar. You can get these at the grocery or pet store. Your cat may even start looking forward to getting its teeth brushed!

KITTENS HAVE 26 BABY TEETH, BUT ADULT CATS HAVE 30 TEETH.

Cats are very neat and groom themselves a lot, but sometimes you might need to give your cat a hand. Most cats love to be brushed. It helps keep them healthy and looking good.

Longhaired cats need to be brushed at least three times a week, but some need brushing everyday. This keeps their fur from getting matted. Shorthaired cats can be brushed once a week and that will be enough to keep shedding under control and reduce hairballs.

Get a cat brush from the pet store to use when grooming your cat. Do not brush near your cat's face or eyes, and be gentle as you brush out tangles in your cat's fur.

Cats rarely need baths, but if your cat does need one, let a professional do it. Most cats really don't like getting wet and can be hard to control.

A cat's nails need to be trimmed every other month or so. Just like baths, it's best to have a professional do the nail trimming. But you could help an adult clip your cat's nails with special trimmers. You can get the trimmers at the pet store. They look like a small pair of pliers.

When you massage your cat's paw, the nail will come out of the sheath. Place the trimmers over the tip

of the nail. Squeeze the handle and a small blade comes down to cut the nail tip. Make sure you only clip the very end of the nail. If you cut down too far, you could hit the vein and cause bleeding. That is why it's so important to have an adult help you.

What's Your Cat Saying?

CAT ON PATROL

Ears are perked showing curiosity.
Paws are planted firmly and confidently on the ground.

CAT READY TO POUNCE

Body is slinking low to the ground, head forward, with tail moving for balance
Smooth body fur displaying confidence.
Forward ears showing assertiveness.
Dilated pupils indicating excitement.
Expression is concentrated.
Back legs are bent, ready for action.

CAT RELAXED AND CONTENT

Whiskers are sensing surrounding area.
Direct eye contact showing trust.
Tail is relaxed, in a downward position.
Eyes are slanted, indicating relaxation.
Ears are attentive.

ANGER OR FEAR

Back is arched high.
Ears are flattened back against head
Tail is fluffed.
Ready to scratch and bite, if approached.

What's Your Cat Saying?

The Tail

* When a cat is angry, excited, or ready to pounce, it energetically swishes its tail.
* When a cat is ready to attack or is feeling curious, it points its tail straight up with the tip curled down.
* A happy cat's tail doesn't move much, or it swishes very slowly.
* When a cat is extremely happy it will hold it's tail as straight as possible.
* An annoyed cat will have a stiff tail with a twitching tip, and a scared or angry cat's tail will arch and bristle.
* A relaxed cat holds its tail low to the ground.

* When a male cat holds his tail bent forward towards his head he is telling everyone that he is king!

Rubbing

* When your cat rubs against you with its body or the side of its face, it is claiming you as its own.
* If it rubs its nose or forehead against you, it is showing you affection.

Whiskers

A happy or curious cat fully extends its whiskers. An irritated or sick cat pulls its whiskers tightly against its face.

Ears

🐾 If a cat's ears are pointed up and moving, it's happy and aware of its surroundings.

🐾 Frightened or defensive cats flatten their ears against their heads.

🐾 Cats that are ready to fight pull their ears back to avoid injury.

Eyes

🐾 When a cat's pupils are large and round, it is frightened or excited. Large pupils allow more light to get into the eye and help the cat see better.

🐾 A cat is curious or happy when its eyes are wide open.

🐾 If a cat's eyes are half closed, it is time to sleep.

🐾 When a cat is lying down with its eyes closed, but its tail is flicking slightly, it is really awake. It's spying on you to see what you're up to!

🐾 When a cat is actually sleeping, its eyes are closed and its tail doesn't move, but it is still alert and will respond if touched.

Patterns

SOLID/SELF:

One single color on the cat's whole body.

AGOUTI:

Several bands of color appear on the cat, with ticking on single hairs.

POINTED:

Points on the ears, legs, and tail are darker than the rest of the body.

PIED:

Splashes of color appear unevenly on the cat's body.

MITTED:

White fur appears on all four of the cat's paws.

Colors

TORTOISESHELL:

A cat that has two or more distinct colors.

TABBY:

The tips of the cat's hair are a different color than the rest of the hair. Spotted, blotchy, or freckled pieces of color appear all over the cat's body. Many tabby cats have stripes like a tiger.

WHITE SPOTTED:

White spotting hides the tabby on some cats. Tabby will only appear in patches on this cat's head and tail, and the rest of the body will be white. The cat is still really a tabby cat.

WHITE:

Some cats are entirely white. A cat with white fur on its face and ears may get sunburned just like a person!

Coat

A cat needs good nutrition in order to have a beautiful, healthy coat. A longhaired cat actually has two layers of fur in its coat, while a shorthaired cat only has one. Some longhaired cats like the Persian can live in colder climates, while most shorthaired cats prefer warmer climates. There is actually a kind of cat called the Sphinx that has no hair and needs to be kept warm. It also needs a bath regularly.

What is a Breed?

People use the word breed to talk about the kinds of animals within a group (like cats). Cat breeds are grouped by color, pattern, body shape, fur length, and personality. All cats that fit in a specific breed have the same look and similar personalities.

Only one percent of the world's cats are "purebred." A purebred cat has parents from the same breed and those parents were also born to cats of the same breed. Purebred cats are considered valuable. Cats that have parents who are not from the same breed are called "moggies." Most cats in the world are moggies.

Which cat breed is right for you? In the next part of the book, you'll learn all about some of the more beautiful, most exotic, and unusual cat breeds. Each cat has a "paw rating" for the amount of time you'll need to spend grooming them. The more paws you see, the more work it will be.

One of the most popular cat breeds, Abyssinians have flexible, muscular bodies and each of their hairs are decorated with light colored bands that mix with dark fur. Abyssinians are athletic and playful. They will run, jump, and do all kinds of tricks to put on a show for their owners. Abysinnians are friendly cats, but they don't like to be held.

Origin: Ethiopia/Egypt
Grooming:
Weight: 4-9 lbs. (1.5-3 kg)
Coat: Shorthair
Color: Rusty, red, blue, and fawn
Personality: Smart, Curious, Brave, Active, Athletic, Playful
Unique Feature: A ring of dark color on the eyelids makes this kitty look like it's wearing makeup.

The American Curl has only been an official breed since 1981. These cats are one of the most affectionate breeds, always cuddling and nuzzling their owners. They are very independent, but like to play (fetch mostly) and check out everything that's happening around them.

Origin: America
Grooming:
Weight: 7-10 lbs. (3-4 kg)
Coat: Longhair
Color: Many different colors
Personality: Energetic, Loving, Very affectionate
Unique Feature: When curls are born their ears are straight, but at seven days the ears begin to curl. They will curl and uncurl until they set permanently at about four months old.

Wirehairs are very curious cats and want to know about everything going on in their owner's life. They are said to know how their owners are feeling.

Origin: America
Grooming: 🐾 🐾 🐾 🐾
Weight: 8-15 lbs. (3-6 kg)
Coat: Longhair
Color: Many different colors
Personality: Quiet, Reserved, Loyal and Loving to owner
Unique Feature: This breed began as a strange mutation in a litter found on a farm in upstate New York in 1966. This kind of change is very rare. What is even more unusual about the Wirehair mutation is that it has only happened in America.

Balinese are a breed of longhaired cats similar to Siamese. They are very talkative and are not for someone who is looking for a quiet kitty. But a Balinese, like a Wirehair, can sense its owner's feelings. They can be very affectionate. They may not be as constantly loving as some other breeds, but they are smart cats who love to clown around.

Origin: America
Grooming:
Weight: 5.5-11 lbs. (2-4 kg)
Coat: Medium length, silky and fine
Color: Seal, blue, lilac, and chocolate points
Personality: Active, Playful, Energetic, Smart, Vocal
Unique Feature: These cats were named after graceful dancers on the island of Bali.

Balinese

This breed of cat is rare and was created when a wild leopard cat mated with a domestic cat. These cats may not be best for kids to own, because some of them can still act wild. But most Bengal's make sweet, playful pets. If you're interested in this breed, ask your vet how to make sure you get a Bengal with a good temperament.

Origin: America
Grooming:
Weight: 6-18 lbs. (2-7 kg)
Coat: Short spotted fur that is thick and soft
Color: Brown tabby, silver, peach, and red
Personality: Playful, Energetic, Curious
Unique Feature: These cats actually like water and sometimes even go swimming!

Birmans have been an official breed in America since 1967. These cats are very dignified, like Siamese and Balinese cats, but are not as active. Birmans like to relax and take it easy. They also like to be adored, and want to show their owner affection, too.

Origin: Burma
Grooming:
Weight: 10-18 lbs. (4-7 kg)
Coat: Medium length and silky
Color: Seal, blue, lilac, and chocolate points
Personality: Sweet, Smart, Quiet, Charming, Easy Going
Unique Feature: All Birmans have white colored paws.

Bombays look like they might belong in the jungle, but they're actually sweet, calm, and really cuddly. The best part is, these cats love kids! They enjoy being a part of the family, learning to play fetch, and can even be trained to go for walks on a leash.

Origin: England
Grooming:
Weight: 8-15 lbs. (3-6 kg)
Coat: Shorthair and glossy
Color: Black
Personality: Loving and Playful
Unique Feature: Gold colored eyes

Burmese cats are very trusting and loyal. They love to play, and continue being active even as adults. A Burmese is one smart cat! They're known for being intelligent, but they don't have good survival instincts. Remember to keep your Burmese inside the house and enjoy its love and affection.

Origin: Burma
Grooming:
Weight: 7-9 lbs. (3-4 kg)
Coat: Shorthair
Color: Sable, champagne, blue, and platinum
Personality: Loving, Loyal, Playful, Active, Vocal
Unique Feature: These cats like to talk, but their natural voices actually sound scratchy, like they have a sore throat.

Burmese

These cats were originally bred as hunters, but today make wonderful pets. Chartreux (pronounced Shar-truse) are quiet, but have a playful side too. They love their owners and like to show affection. A Chartreux is a good athlete even though its legs don't look big enough for its body.

Origin: France
Grooming:
Weight: 9-12 lbs. (3-4.5 kg)
Coat: Double coat of Shorthair that shouldn't be brushed.
Color: Copper, gold, and blue
Personality: Smart, Quiet, Easy Going, Loving, Playful, Active
Unique Feature: These cats were originally bred by monks in the French Alps.

These cats are similar to Siamese, but are a separate breed. They have sleek bodies, very short hair, and large ears. Colorpoint Shorthairs are talkative and playful. They are not shy and really like attention. This breed would be a good choice if you have allergies (they have almost no dander).

Origin: America/Thailand
Grooming:
Weight: 7-9 lbs. (3-4 kg)
Coat: Shorthair
Color: 16 different point colors, including cream, blue, and red
Personality: Smart, Social, Playful, Active
Unique Feature: Beautiful blue eyes

The Cornish and Devon Rex are very athletic kitties. These cats can run, jump, and balance in the craziest places. They are small cats that can be real clowns—you might even find a Rex on the ceiling fan! They give and need a lot of attention. These cats look like aliens because of their large eyes and ears, but they're really sweet cats who love to cuddle. They don't shed very much and their coats are light, so you may find your Rex relaxing in warm places (like on top of a computer).

Origin: England
Grooming:
Weight: 5.5-10 lbs. (2-4 kg)
Coat: Shorthair (feels like velvet)
Color: Many different colors
Personality: Active, Playful, Loving
Unique Feature: The Devon and Cornish Rex may want your dinner. These cats are beggars for people food.

These cats were worshipped by the Egyptians and are loved by many people today for their unique spotted coat and sparkling, green eyes. The Mau has a nice look and a beautiful personality. Maus are very loyal to their families. These cats like being with their owners, but they like to be alone, too. They don't talk a lot and like to relax.

Origin: Egypt
Grooming:
Weight: 5.5-11 lbs. (2-4 kg)
Coat: Shorthair
Color: Silver, bronze, smoke, blue, and black
Personality: Smart, Quiet, Easy Going
Unique Feature: The Mau makes different sounds called "chortling."

These cats are like Persians, but they have less hair and don't need as much grooming. They are really relaxed cats, but they can be playful and always enjoy cuddling.

Origin: America
Grooming:
Weight: 9-12 lbs. (3-4.5 kg)
Coat: Shorthair (thick fur)
Color: Many different colors
Personality: Easy Going, Loving, Quiet
Unique Feature: The thick fur coat makes them look for cool areas of the house.

These cats won't be happy unless they're getting a lot of attention from their owners. They're very loyal, but need a lot of love. Your Havana will be a quiet, sweet, and playful friend. Havanas can learn to play fetch and to go for walks on a leash.

Origin: America
Grooming:
Weight: 8-10 lbs. (3-4 kg)
Coat: Shorthair
Color: Chocolate brown
Personality: Smart, Loyal, Loving, Playful, Quiet
Unique Feature: This cat's purr is so loud that their bodies vibrate!

Havana Brown

Japanese Bobtails are a symbol of good luck in Japan. As pets, they're loving, curious, and, smart. They are usually very healthy cats and take good care of themselves. These cats are talkers and make unusual voice sounds sometimes called "singing."

Origin: Japan
Grooming:
Weight: 5.5-9 lbs. (2-4 kg)
Coat: Medium length
Color: Many different colors
Personality: Smart, Active, Vocal
Unique Feature: These kittens are born with bobtails and never without tail or with full-length tails.

The Javanese is like the Balinese, but more colorful. Javanese get used to your daily routine and they will talk to you, reminding you when it's time to eat, sleep, and play with them. These cats enjoy being a part of everything their owners do. They also like to play and can open drawers to find things they want.

Origin: America
Grooming:
Weight: 7-9 lbs. (3-4 kg)
Coat: Medium length
Color: Many different colors
Personality: Playful, Active, Loving, Smart
Unique Feature: Javanese love to eat. Make sure your cat is very active, or it will start to gain weight.

Javanese

Korats are considered good luck in their native Thailand. These cats have a high place in that culture, and they like to be pampered. These cats like to have their owners to themselves, but they will get along with other pets. They like to sit on your shoulder or lay in your lap.

Origin: Thailand
Grooming:
Weight: 5.5-11 lbs. (2-4 kg)
Coat: Shorthair
Color: Silver tipped fur (makes the cat look shiny)
Personality: Energetic, Loving, Playful
Unique Feature: Korats have a very good sense of smell, eyesight, and hearing. They don't like loud noises.

There are a lot of legends about this breed. Some say that Maine Coons came to America with sailors. This cat's long, thick coat of fur is perfect for cold weather. Coons are kind and loving pets. They can get quite large for a cat.

Origin: America
Grooming:
Weight: 9-20 lbs. (4-7.5 kg)
Coat: Longhair, thick with bushy tails
Color: Many different colors
Personality: Loving, Quiet, Smart
Unique Feature: Coon cats can be good swimmers because their coats are water-resistant.

Manx come from an island located between England and Ireland. Like the Maine Coon, there are a lot of stories surrounding these cats. The stories revolve around their great personalities. The Manx is a nice mix of fun, playfulness, love, and loyalty.

Origin: England
Grooming:
Weight: 9-12 lbs. (3-4.5 kg)
Coat: Shorthair or Longhair
Color: Many different colors
Personality: Active, Playful, Loving, Loyal, Smart
Unique Feature: These cats don't have tails!

Ocicats were bred to look wild, but to have the traits of domestic cats. They have beautiful, spotted coats and the athletic bodies, like wild cats, but they are very friendly. They get along with everyone and other pets.

Origin: America
Grooming:
Weight: 5.5-14 lbs. (2-5 kg)
Coat: Shorthair
Color: Chocolate, blue, lavender, and silver mixtures
Personality: Loving, Friendly, Active, Playful, Smart
Unique Feature: Ocicats can be trained to respond to voice commands.

Ocicat

Persians are ancient cats who rode camels across deserts with their owners. Today they have become one of the most popular cat breeds. Many people consider their long, silky coats very beautiful. These cats have sweet personalities too.

Origin: Persia
Grooming: 🐾 🐾 🐾 🐾 🐾
Weight: 10-11 lbs. (4-5 kg)
Coat: Longhair
Color: Many different colors
Personality: Sweet, Calm, and Loving
Unique Feature: They have a reputation for being a very relaxed breed of cat, so don't expect your Persian to be very active.

The Ragdoll gets its name from its favorite activity, which is lying around in its owners arms or lap. These cats are real sweethearts, and aren't very active. Ragdolls are a good choice for houses that have kids, older people, or other pets. They make friends with everyone!

Origin: America
Grooming:
Weight: 10-19 lbs. (4-7 kg)
Coat: Shorthair, thick
Color: Brown, blue, chocolate, lilac
Personality: Clam, Quiet, Sweet, Loving, Friendly
Unique Feature: Ragdolls are one of the sweetest and most docile cats anywhere.

Ragdoll

Russian Blues are known for their beautiful blue coats with shiny, silver tipped hair. Blues are great for busy homes. They don't need grooming and keep themselves entertained. They don't usually like strangers and might hide.

Origin: Russia
Grooming:
Weight: 6-8 lbs. (2-3 kg)
Coat: Longhair
Color: Blue
Personality: Smart, Quiet, Loyal
Unique Feature: They like the same routine every day and need a clean litter box.

The reason this cat is called the Scottish Fold is that its ears fold over when it's a kitten. Sometimes the ears don't fold and simply stay straight. The best part is that no one really knows why. The mystery about this cat is part of its appeal.

Origin: Scotland
Grooming:
Weight: 5.5-13 lbs. (2-5 kg)
Coat: Shorthair
Color: Many different colors
Personality: Quiet, Sweet, Loving, Calm
Unique Feature: It has to be the ears!

In Thailand, Siamese used to be very valuable, so only royalty could own them. The first Siamese cat in America lived in the White House! They talk all the time with raspy voices. Many people who have Siamese cats say they make wonderful companions. However, they do have a reputation for having unpleasant personalities.

Origin: Thailand (Once called Siam)
Grooming:
Weight: 5-10 lbs. (2-4 kg)
Coat: Shorthair (close to the body)
Color: Light colored fur
Personality: Vocal, Demanding, Loving, Playful
Unique Feature: Slim body, long neck, and bright blue eyes.

Siamese

Siberians have very strong personalities. They like to play and get into anything and everything. They are good athletes, so you might find your Siberian on top of the fridge.

Origin: Russia
Grooming: 🐾 🐾
Weight: 15-20 lbs. (6-7.5 kg)
Coat: Medium length
Color: Many different colors
Personality: Playful, Active, Loyal
Unique Feature: Siberians are the national cat of Russia.

Singapuras are smaller than average cats. They love following their owners everywhere. They are smart and like to help their human friends.

Origin: Singapore
Grooming: 🐾
Weight: 4-9 lbs. (1.5-4 kg)
Coat: Shorthair
Color: Dark brown
Personality: Playful, Smart, Loving
Unique Feature: Singapuras have very large eyes and ears.

Somalis look like they might be wild mountain cats, but they're very content climbing all over the furniture and you. These cats are very active and love to play. This is probably because Somalis are related to Abyssinians. Both breeds have a curious and fun personality.

Origin: America
Grooming: 🐾🐾🐾
Weight: 8-10 lbs. (3.6-4.5 kg)
Coat: Longhair
Color: Red, blue, ruddy, fawn mixtures
Personality: Smart, Playful, Active
Unique Feature: These cats are sometimes called "fox cats" because they look a bit like foxes.

Somali

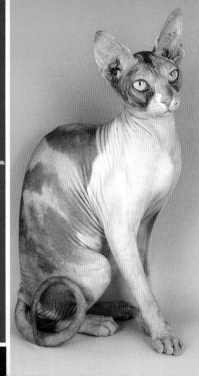

The Sphinx is full of energy and playfulness, and they love to put on a show for their owners. They are very loving, so you might find it under your covers snuggled up close to you. Sphinxes are snugglers not just because they're loving, but because they get cold easily.

Origin: Canada
Grooming:
Weight: 7-15 lbs. (3-6 kg)
Coat: Hairless. Requires a bath every couple of days.
Color: Many different colors
Personality: Active, Playful, Loving, Smart
Unique Feature: They don't have any hair! These cats have a very soft "down" on their bodies. Also, these cats don't mind the water.

Turkish Angoras were once thought to be extinct, but more have been imported from their home country of Turkey. While considered really beautiful, Angoras are also intelligent, graceful, and playful. Your Angora might not like to cuddle, but it will be a devoted friend.

Origin: Turkey
Grooming:
Weight: 5-11 lbs. (2-4 kg)
Coat: Longhair, silky
Color: Many different colors
Personality: Active, Playful, Loving, Loyal, Smart
Unique Feature: These cats have long bodies and pointed ears.

Everywhere Cats

C ats are wonderful, loving friends who will be a clown and play kitty games with you. It's very important to research the different breeds and personalities. Your new cat will be with you a long time. If you want more information about cats, here are a few places to look into:

The Cat Fancier's Association
P.O. Box 1005, Manasquan, NJ 08736 USA
Ph-(732) 528-9797 Fax-(732) 528-7391

The TICA Executive Office
P.O. Box 2684, Harlingen, TX 78552 USA
Ph-(956) 428-8046   Fax-(956)428-8047

Cats International
193 Granville Road
Cedarburg, WI 53012 USA